1000
SONGS
OVER
THE
MOON

1000
songs over the moon

minimal poems

cmbzamora

fpark

"goodbye."

27 August | 2 am

fpark

and you set
your eyes

to the skies,
to the realm

of silence.

spark

"what about goodbye?"

postlude:

no matter how
close we can be,

my earnest whisper
to the heavens,

you will still
remain as *distant* as

a thousand songs
over the moon.

i admit that i am still looking
for you in all versions of you
the you that i worshipped in
my memories the immaculate
the loving the brave yet like
you that is real in my heart the
pain of dissolution is the pain
i always find in every single
you embraced by my goodbyes

6 October | 9:14 pm

since we set sail upon
our own separate times:

the dissipating chances
and the waning of smiles, as

the vastness of the present
grows ever more vast.

6 October | 8:19 pm

do you still
remember me?

6 October | 8:27 pm

movement 4:

i presumed then, the time
beside you knows how
to endure and wait

i know that they will be brought to your feet
by the crashing waves of the sea, gandering
with the sands where you are standing

there on the shore that no one knows
where, and they will etch on the cheeks
of the water my counting of a thousand

centuries of you and beyond, how it slipped
from consciousness that you may fade away
as fast as the flutter of the eyelids.

only with the purl
of this ambrosia are

my fragments being swept,
momentarily kept

in the bosom of all things,
in the womb of the pages

telling a thousand versions
of you and beyond;

what is the meaning
of my passing but a humble

blink of an eye

28 December | 9:55 pm

the countless neat glasses
of bourbon are responding

to the senses. now, holding
another one. rotating,

remembering your mien
during our last meeting;

even the placement
of moles on your body,

their number, their measure,
which one time i traced

under the pretense that
they are the stars.

movement 3:

profound,
without

end,
untainted.

4 July | 12:07 am

the silence:

your skin
of porcelain

that gathered
starlights;

the lips
that only

in dreams
could find

the most
solemn kiss.

the twine
of the braids

encircling
your head;

the graceful
bend of your

eyelashes.

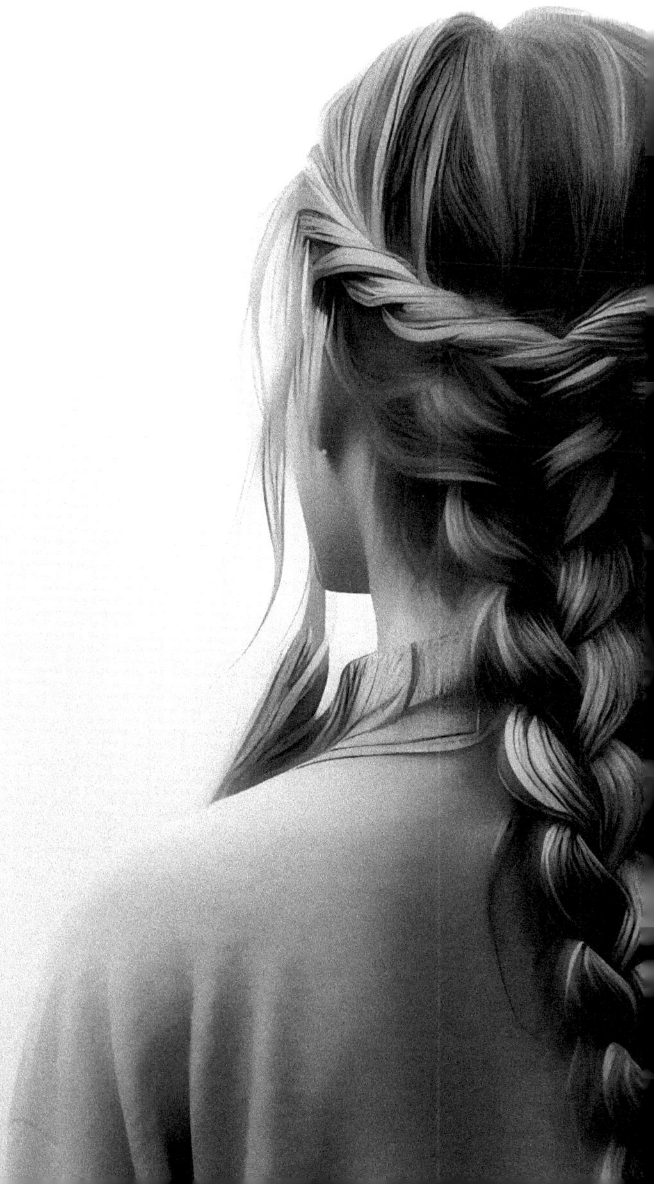

since the tongue
is tied and

no words yet
want to escape,

i studied you
in secret

concealed by
the book i held

in my hand.

i remained
silent with

each passing
second:

listening to
her slow

rhythmic
breathing.

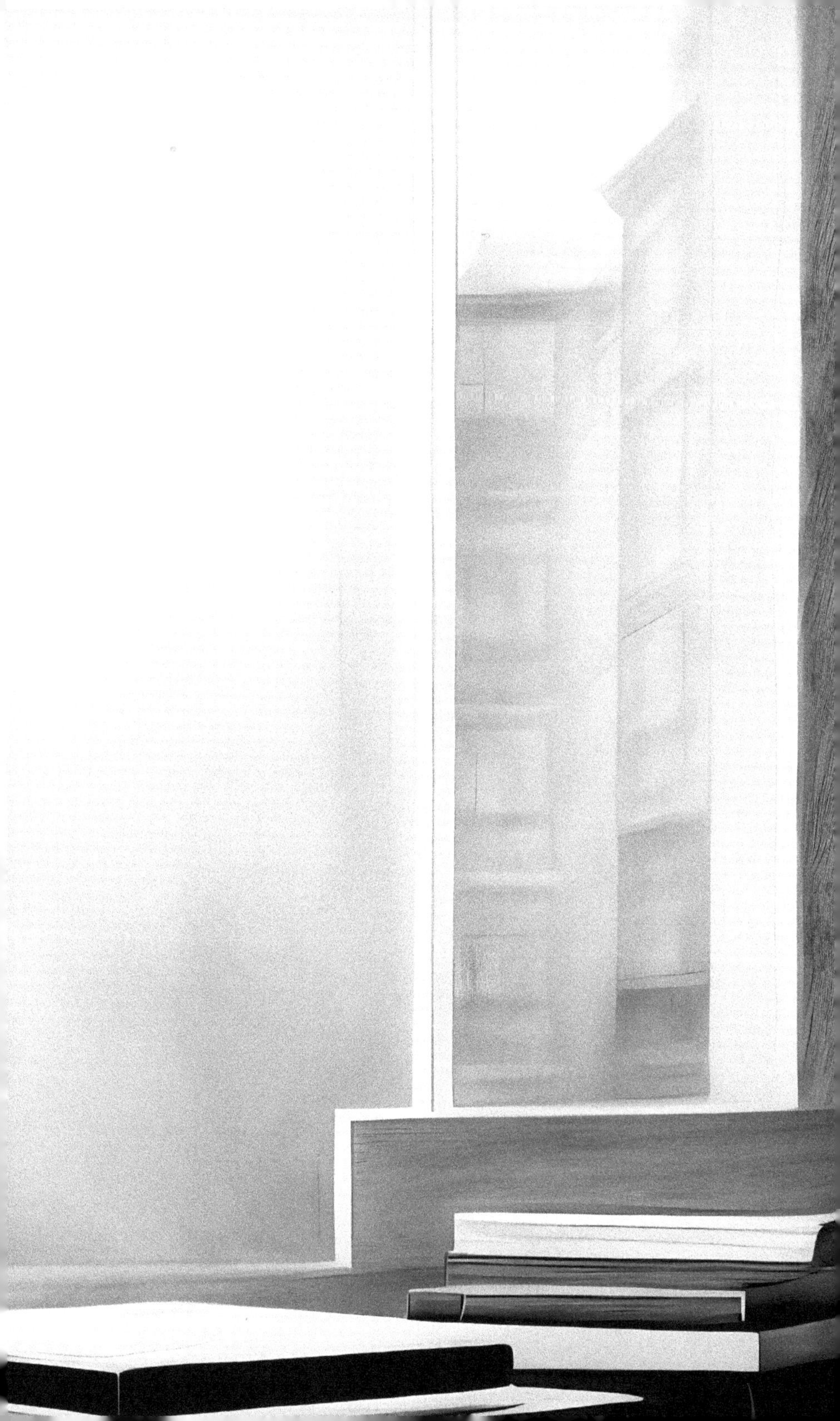

with haste
i turned to you,

praying that
i would catch

a faint moment
when your eyes

would fix a gaze
into mine; but

they did *not*.

"silence."

so i gently
pulled the chair

in front of you.
its feet only

seemed to groan,
then a long

squeak echoed
through the hall.

13 March | 11:48 pm

"may i sit
beside you?"

i asked.
but you only

said nothing
not even

a glance
nor a nod

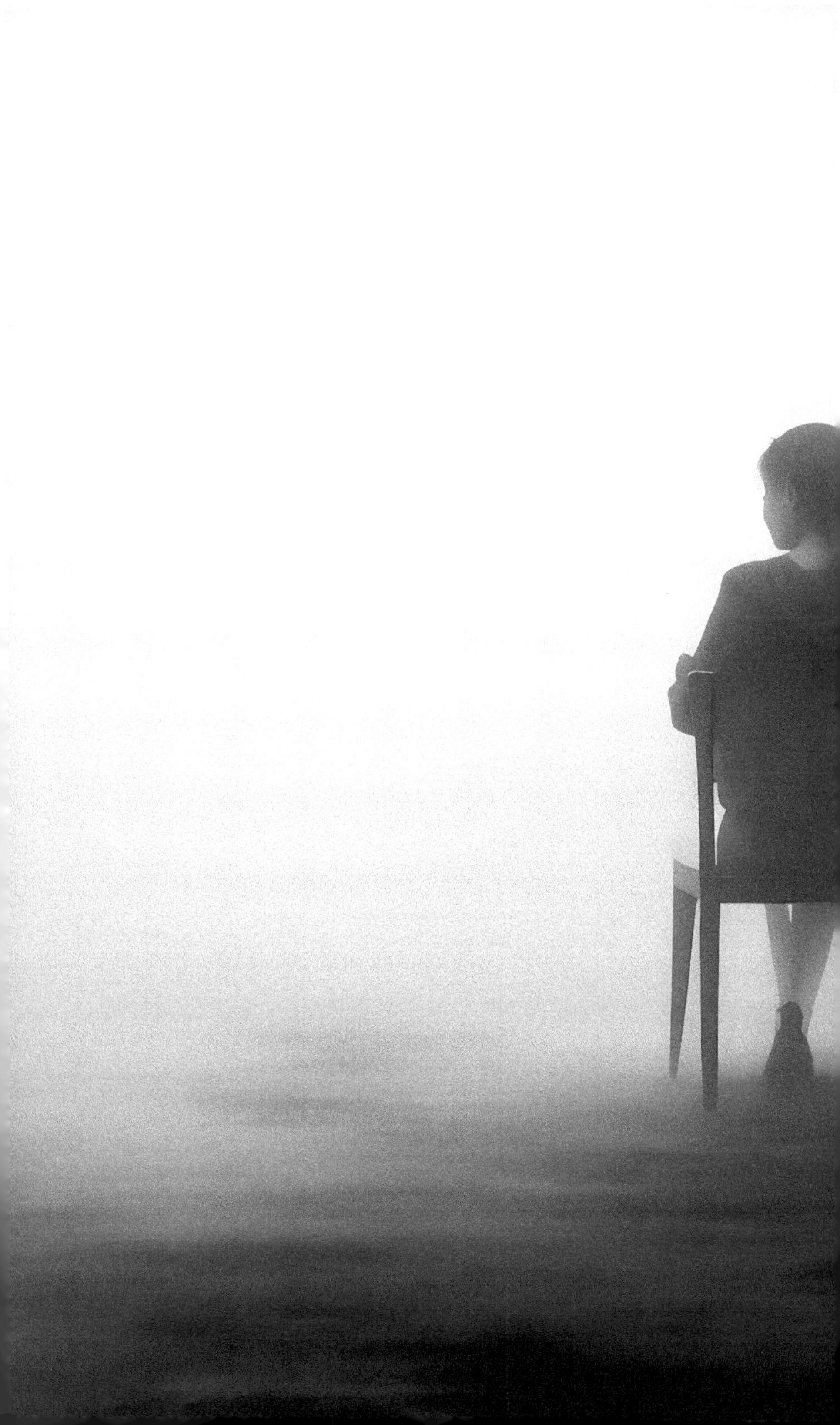

i crossed
the distance

between us.
just a few

meters
nonetheless,

but our hearts
seem to stand

on two far ends
of a world

13 March | 11:27 pm

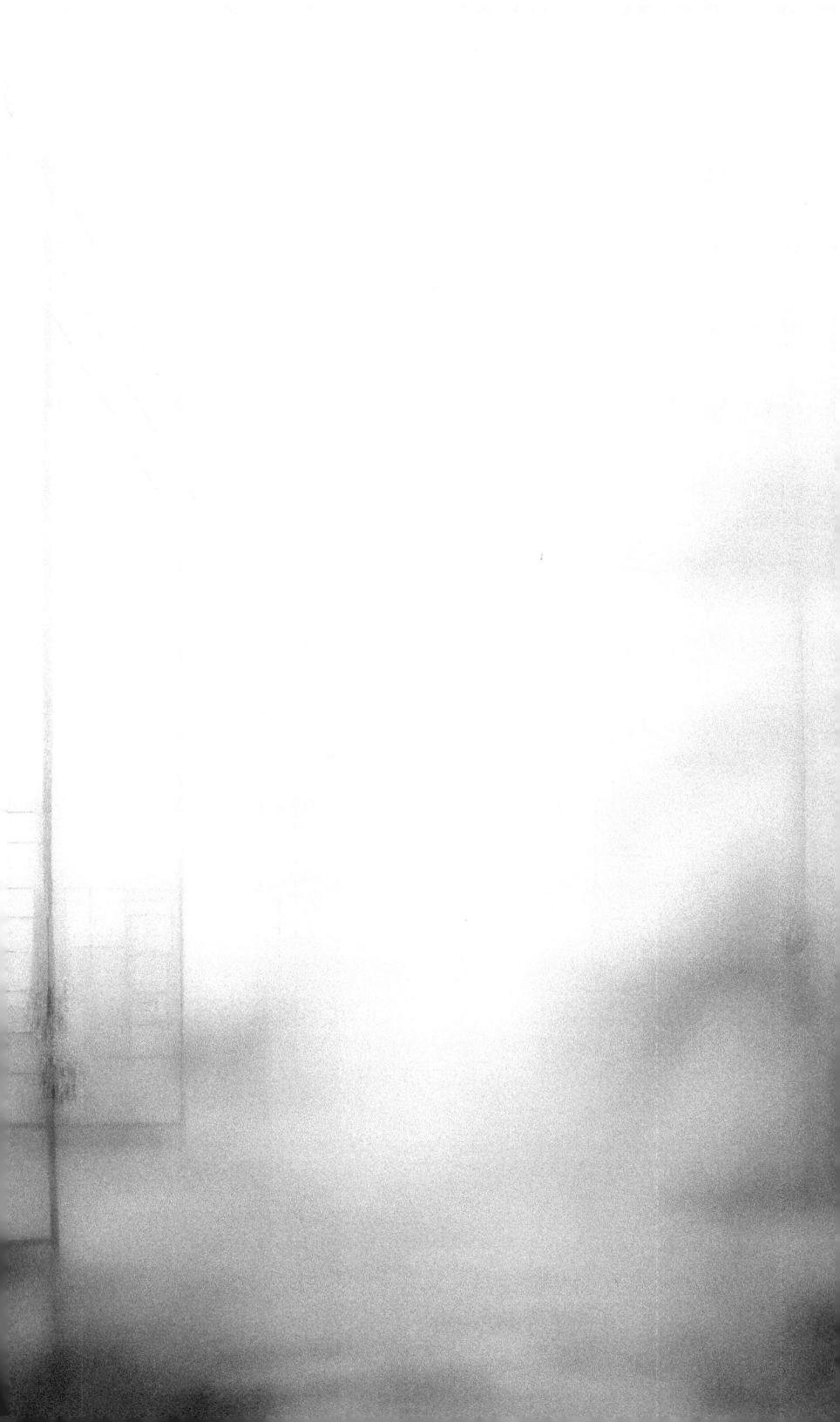

except for
Nietzche,

you're only
enjoying

the company
of a table

and three
empty chairs.

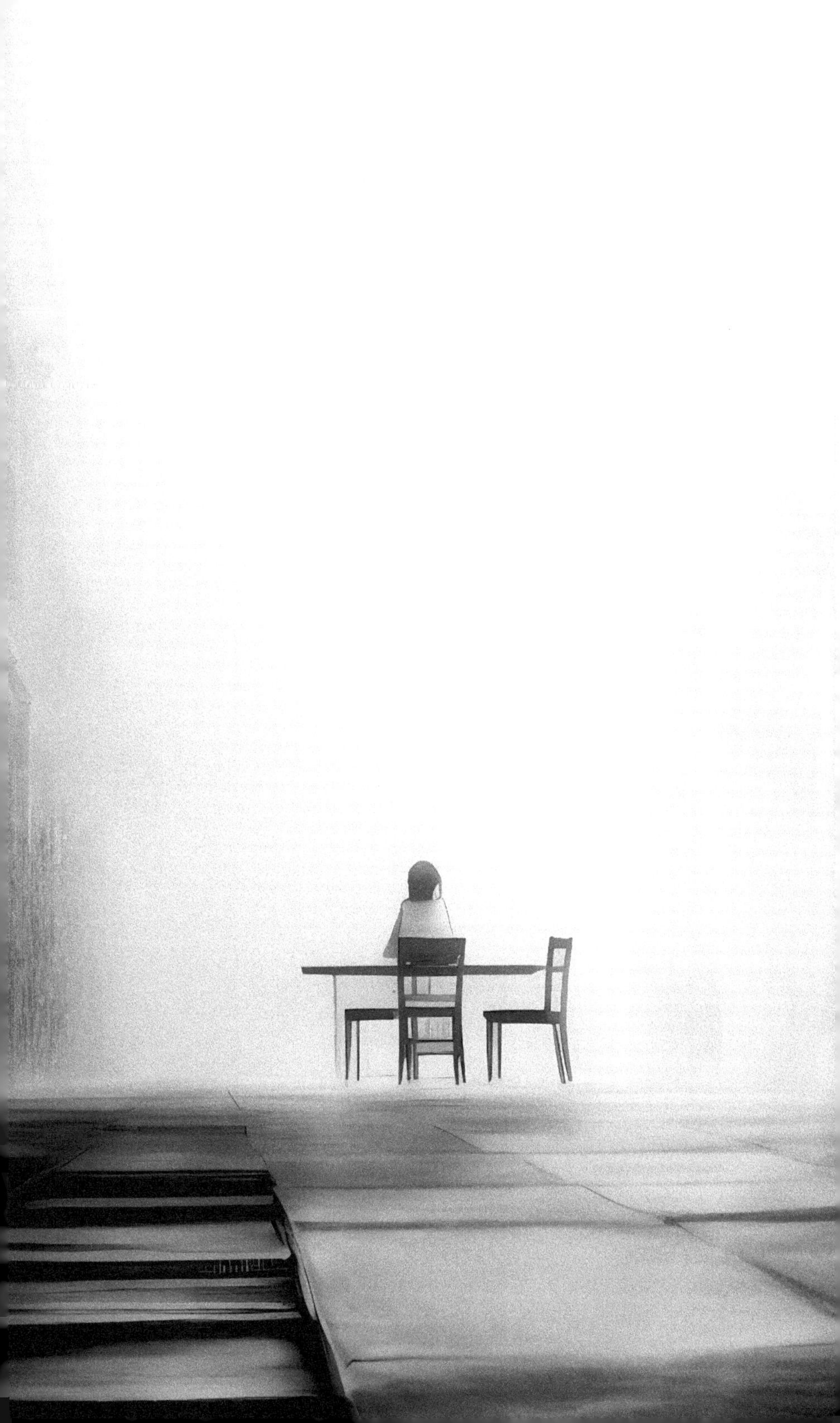

i can only
see you hazily

from where
i am standing,

through a small
dusty crevice

the books
permit.

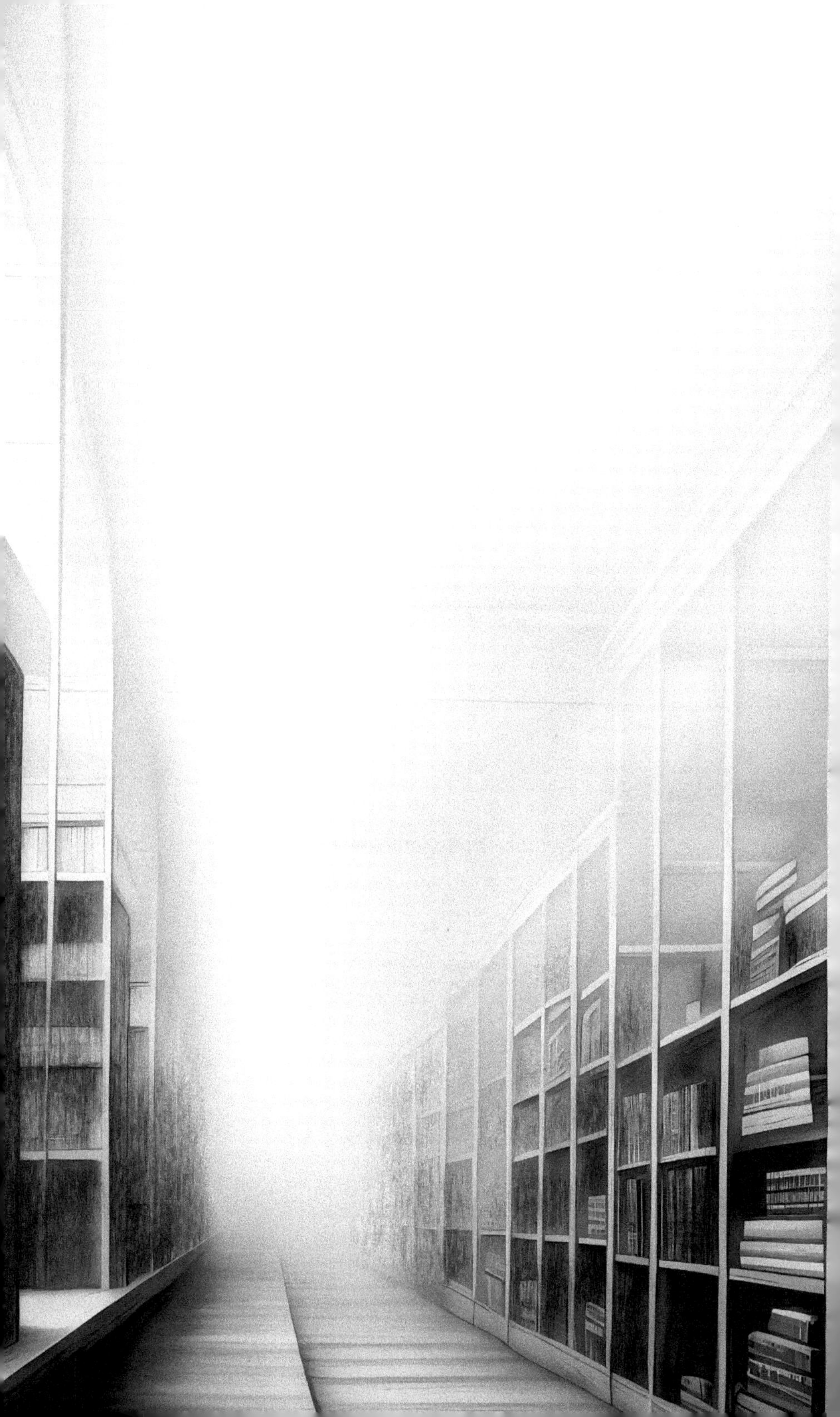

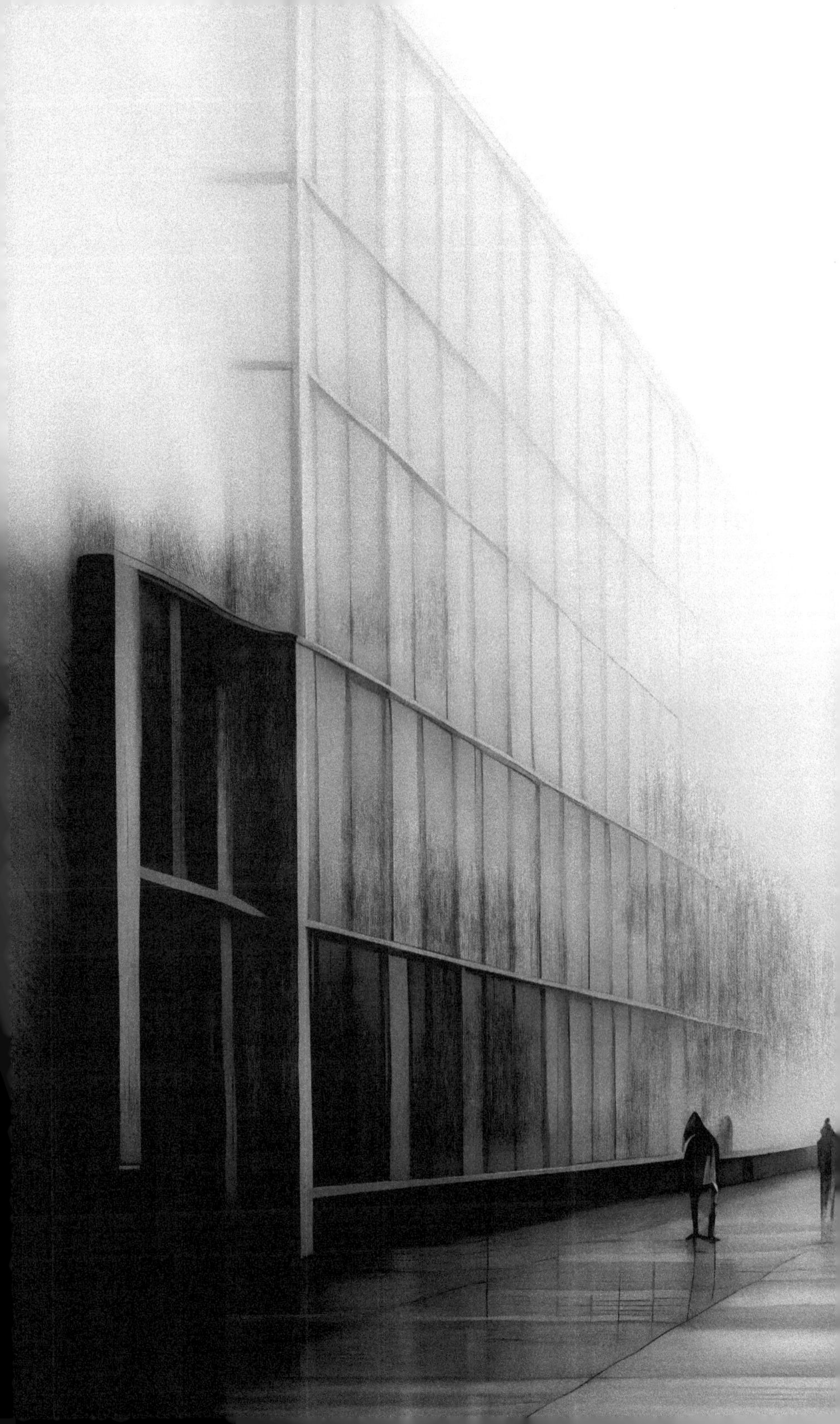

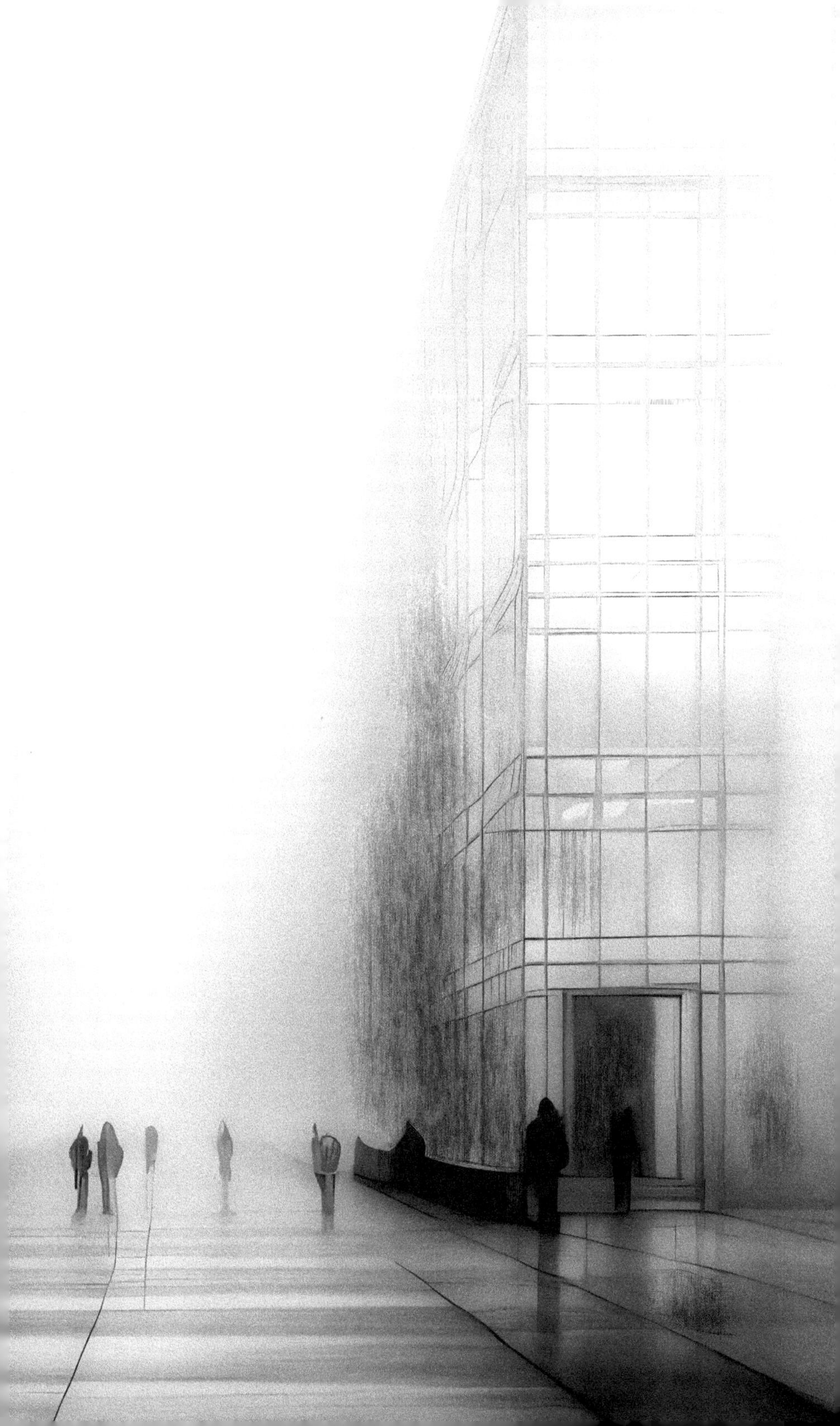

"yesterday,

i stumbled upon
a bookstore.

i suddenly
found myself

thinking of you."

5 March | 11:34 am

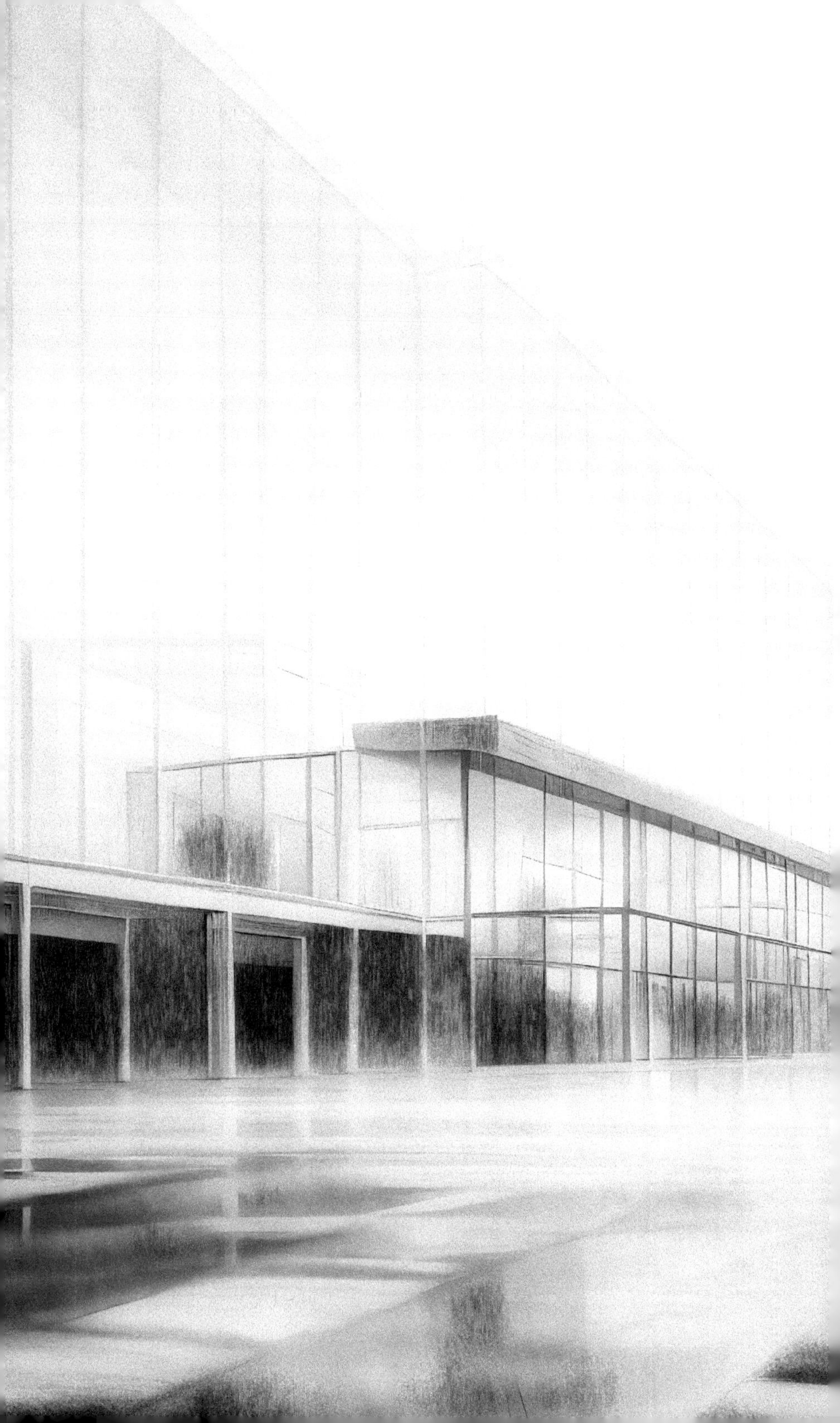

"are
you
busy?"

5 March | 11:20 am

movement 2:

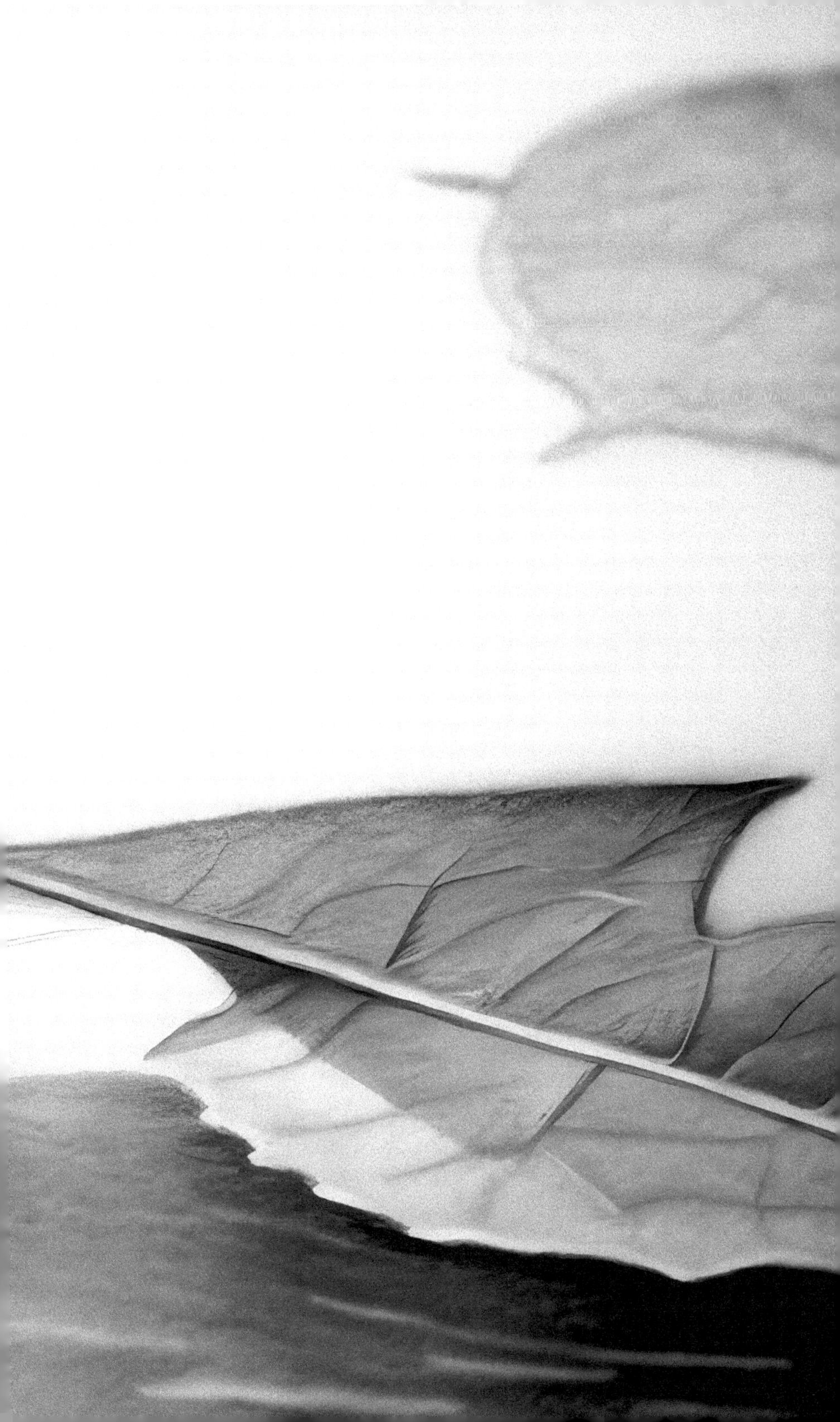

the fallen leaf wrinkled
the face of a puddle

if these worlds
will ever find you,

will their enigma
echo the mystery

you always unravel
with every coming

of the rain?

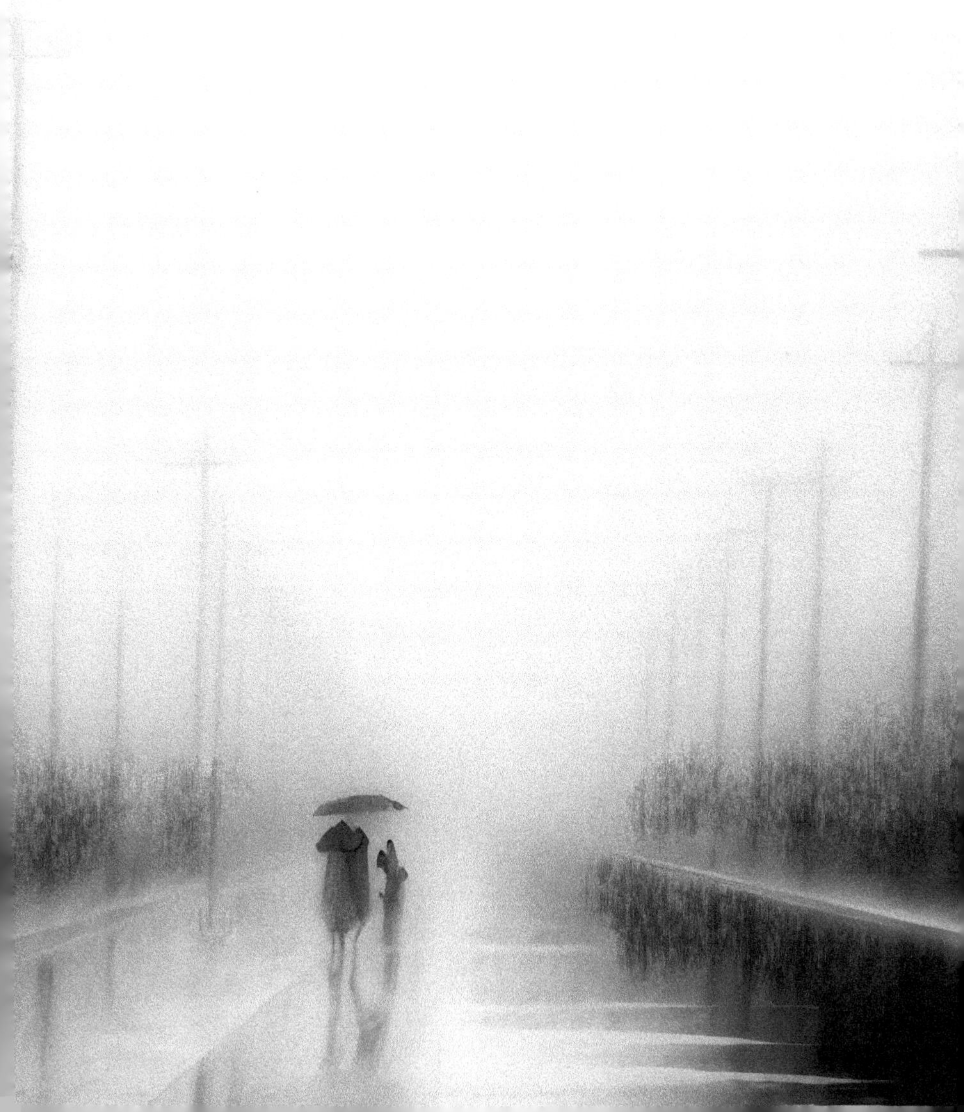

rainwater is the blood
of the gallant lake

imprisoned in the heart
of each drop of ink

that conceives and forges
all the worlds of poems

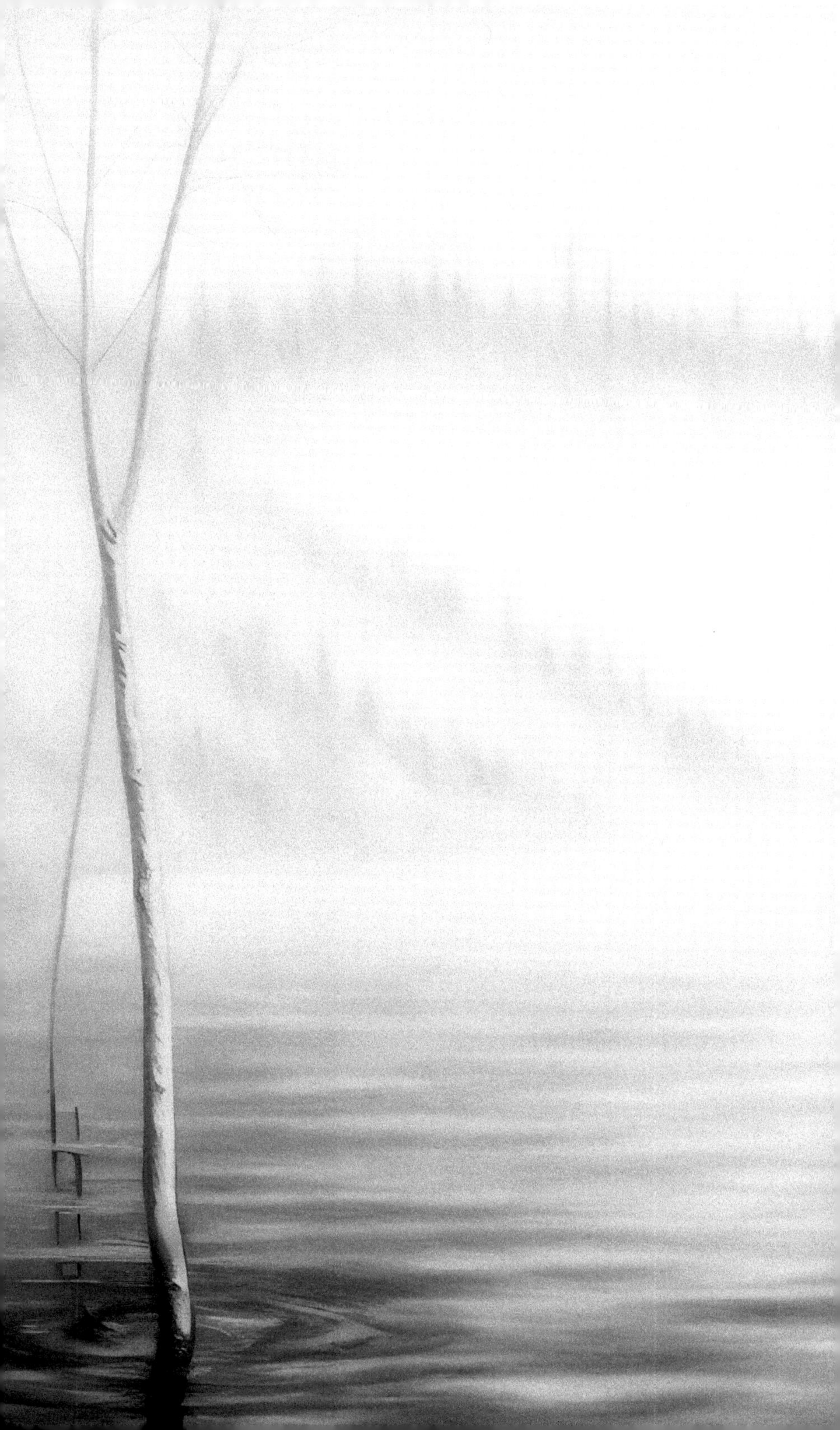

the waves of your inexistence
are dragging me into my abyss
clenched in your palm

is the spark of the stars
that one by one evanesce
you wove the darkness

the creator of this universe
which gradually disentangles
coheres combines with the rain

facing the keyboard
of skinny songs

on fingertips linger
the shape of your lips,

the hues of departure;
burning down

in the intricate downpour
that seldom descends

concurrent with the flow
is each passing moment

draining into the sink
streaming into the creek

carrying along
a paper boat

of particles and words
gushing from the chest

it is raining
outside

Apt. 2 | 31 August | 12:25 nn

movement 1:

iii
what tune will it be
for all tomorrows

if in their glimpse
into an existence
they find emptiness,

a hollow space
that only knows
how to breath (grieve)

with the passing
of a thousand
memories

Apt. 2 | 20 July | 10:14 am

ii
what can disperse,
in time,
the clouds

that shroud
the light of the sun,
or the moon, or even

the stars
that always
smile

upon us?

i

what light can part
the morning
from night,

happiness
from every sorrow
within a soul,

every pulse of life
between the first
and last grain

of rain?

uhs

Hiding
beneath

a pair
of glasses

is the
beautiful

gentle
soul

prelude:

how many poems
must i still need

to adorn
with melodies

so i may *reach* you
(even just the gentlest

touch upon your skin)
through my songs

calamba exit | 1 September | 1 am

Preface

The year was disquieting when these were all written. *Nanay*—my grandma—passed on, taking her epic stories with her. My friend *Rodge* followed not long after. And as the year ended, I had my last real conversation with someone I deeply hold dear in my heart and memories. Though she remains present, she's somewhere I can't reach.

I built this sanctuary for them, at least a semblance of one, to keep my recollections of them from fading further and to allow me to return. The words in this sanctuary are sparse. After all, sanctuaries need their silence.

Contents

prelude : 21
movement 1 : 33
movement 2 : 51
movement 3 : 89
movement 4 : 101
postlude : 113

"*The past, again and again.*"

—Maj. Jack Celliers, *Merry Christmas Mr. Lawrence* (1983)

"*...Lebens muß dir wiederkommen, und alles in dersel ben Reihe und Folge* (life must recur to you, and everything in the same order and sequence)...."

—Friedrich Nietzsche, *Die frölich Wissenchaft* (1882)

"*...život, který zmizí jednou provždy, který se nenavrátí, je podoben stínu, je bez váhy, je předem mrtvý a byl-li strašný, krásný, vznešený, ta hrůza, vznešenost čí krása nic neznamenají* (life, which vanishes once and for all, which does not return, is like a shadow, weightless, dead in advance and whether it was terrible, beautiful, or sublime, that horror, sublimity, or beauty mean nothing)."

—Milan Kundera, *Nesnesitelná lehkost bytí* (1985)

"*Silence is the perfectest herald of joy.*"

—William Shakespeare, *Much Ado About Nothing* (1623)

*for the
interludes*

*between
us*

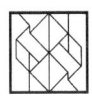

1000 SONGS OVER THE MOON

Copyright © 2024 christian marvin b. zamora

All rights reserved. No part of this book may be reproduced, distributed, or transmitted in any form or by any means, electronic or mechanical, including photocopying, recording, or by any information storage and retrieval system without the written permission of the author.

The images in this book were created with the assistance of artificial intelligence technology, enhancing on an original image provided by the author without any artist name prompt. The author then further altered these images to produce the final illustrations.

```
ISBN 978-621-06-1653-8 (hbd)
ISBN 978-621-06-1702-3 (pbk)
```

National Library of the Philippines CIP Data
Recommended entry:

    Zamora, Christian Marvin B.
        1000 songs over the moon: minimal poems / Christian Marvin B. Zamora. — First edition. — Silang, Cavite : CMBZamora, 2024, c2024.
        pages; cm

        ISBN 978-621-06-1653-8 (hbd)
        ISBN 978-621-06-1702-3 (pbk)

        1. Philippine poetry (English).   I. Title.

899.2101   PR9550.6   2024   P420240167

First edition, 2024.

Published by
cmbzamora
Silang, Cavite, Philippines 4118
cmbzamora@gmail.com

1000
songs over
the moon

minimal poems

cmbzamora

1000
SONGS
OVER
THE
MOON

Milton Keynes UK
Ingram Content Group UK Ltd.
UKHW051024100924
447858UK00026B/77/J